Published by Withington & Co. LLC

Withington & Co. LLC
16067 NW Rondos Dr.
Portland, OR USA 97229-9239

ISBN: 979-8-9945334-5-1

Tagalog-English Words for Children

Jeanette Withington
Edith Withington

head - ulo
oo-loh

eyes - mata
mah-tah

nose - ilong
ee-long

lips - bibig
bee-big

Body Parts
Katawan
ka-tah-wan

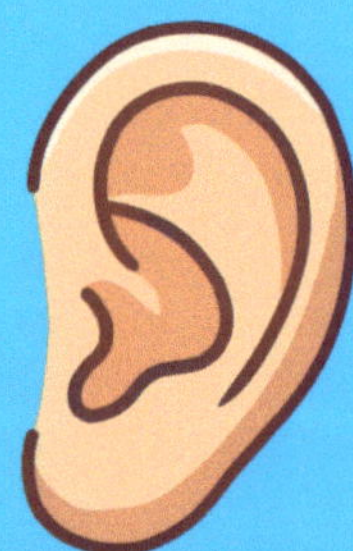

ear - tainga
tah-ee-ngah

hair - buhok
boo-hook

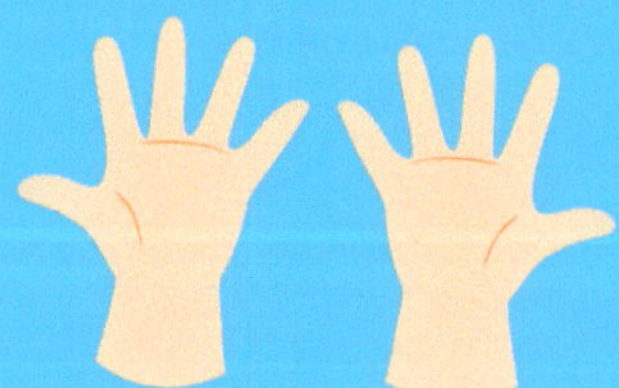

hands - kamay
kah-my

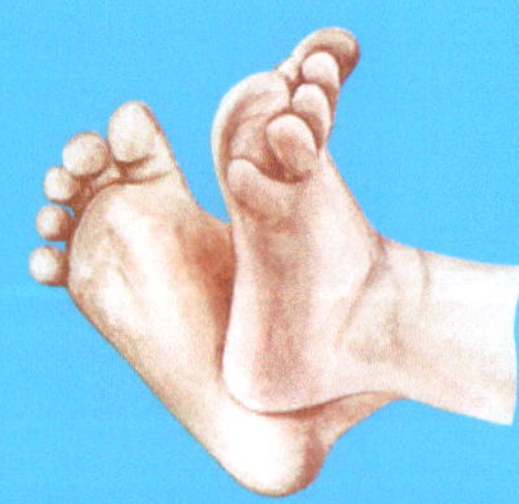

feet - paa
pah-ah

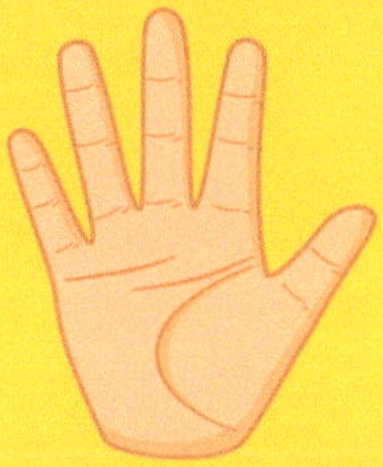

fingers - daliri
dah-lee-ree

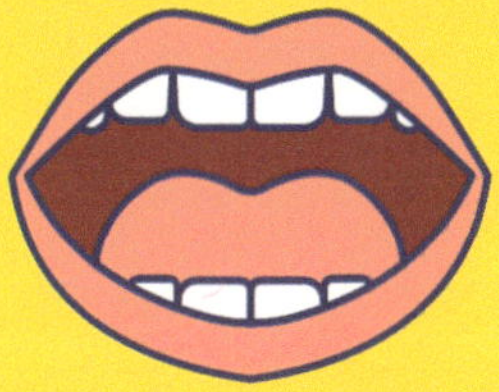

mouth - bunganga
boo-nga-ngah

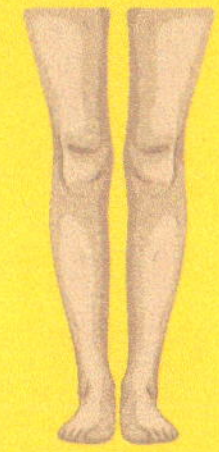

legs - binti
bin-tee

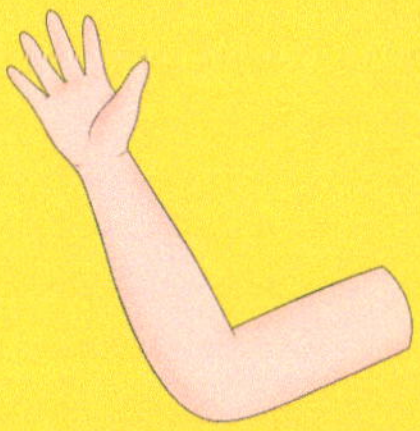

arm - braso
brah-so

Body Parts
Katawan
ka-tah-wan

stomach - tyan
tee-yahn

tongue - dila
dee-lah

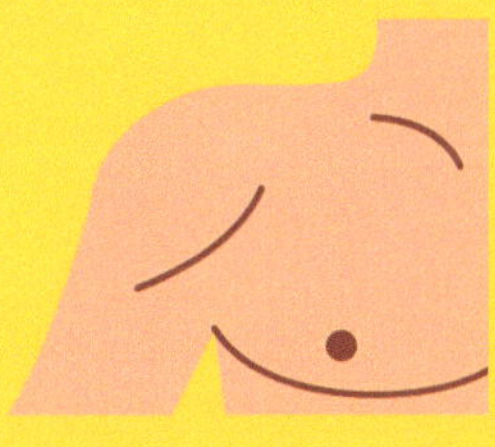

shoulder - balikat
bah-lee-kat

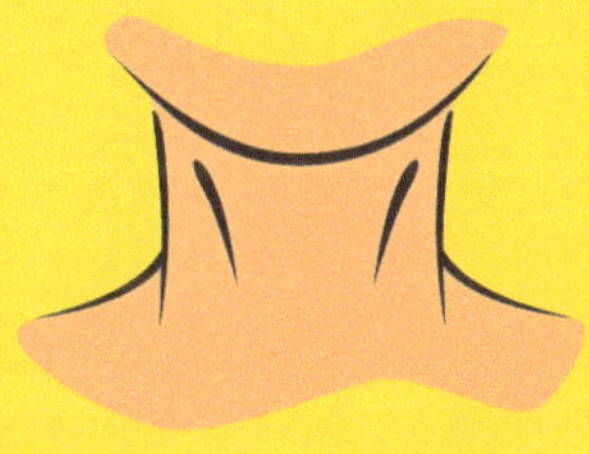

neck - leeg
leh-eg

zebra - sebra
seh-bra

elephant - elepante
eh-leh-pan-teh

snake - ahas
ah-has

crocodile - buwaya
boo-wah-yah

Animals
Hayop
ha-yoop

turtle - pagong
pah-gong

tiger - tigre
tee-greh

monkey - unggoy
oon-goy

giraffe - dyirap
jee-rahp

pig - baboy
bah-boy

horse - kabayo
kah-bah-yoh

duck - pato
pah-toh

mouse - daga
dah-gah

Animals
Hayop
ha-yoop

owl - kuwago
koo-wah-goh

cow - baka
bah-kah

buffalo - kalabaw
kah-lah-baw

chicken - manok
mah-nok

ant - langgam
lang-gahm

ladybug - kulisap
koo-lee-sap

bee - bubuyog
boo-boo-yog

grasshopper -
tipaklong
tee-pahk-long

Insects
Insekto
in-sek-toh

butterfly - paruparo
pah-roo-pah-roh

beetle- salagubang
sa-la-goo-bang

dragonfly - tutubi
too-too-bee

mosquito - lamok
lah-mohk

left - kaliwa
kah-lee-wah

right - kanan
kah-nahn

straight - deretso
deh-reh-tso

far - malayo
mah-lah-yoh

Directions & Places
Direksyon at Lugar
dee-rek-see-yon at loo-gar

up - taas
tah-ahs

exit - labasan
lah-bah-san

parking - paradahan
pa-rah-da-han

down - baba
bah-bah

rice - kanin
kah-nin

main dish - ulam
oo-lahm

steak - bistek
bis-tek

vegetables - gulay
goo-lie

Food & Drink
Pagkain at Inumin
pag-kah-in at ee-no-min

fish - isda
ees-dah

coffee - kape
kah-peh

milk - gatas
gah-tas

water - tubig
too-big

papaya - papaya
pa-pah-yah

orange - dalanghita
dah-lahng-hee-tah

mango - mangga
man-gah

coconut - niyog
nee-yog

Fruits
Prutas
pro-tas

banana - saging
sah-ging

avocado - abokado
ah-boh-kah-doh

pineapple - pinya
peen-yah

apple - mansanas
man-sah-nas

table - mesa
meh-sa

fan - bentilador
ben-tee-lah-dor

bed - kama
kah-mah

television -
telebisyon
teh-leh-bis-yon

Home
Gamit sa Bahay
gah-meet sah
bah-hi

chair - upuan
oo-poh-an

lamp - ilaw
ee-law

mirror - salamin
sah-lah-min

couch - sopa
so-pah

plate - plato
pla-toh

knife - kutsilyo
kut-sil-yoh

pot - kaldero
kal-deh-roh

pan - palayok
pa-lah-yok

Kitchen
Kusina
koo-see-na

oven - hurno
hoor-no

spoon - kutsara
koot-sah-rah

mug - tasa
tah-sah

kettle - takure
tah-koo-reh

shampoo - shampo
sham-poo

toothbrush - sipilyo
see-pil-yoh

towel - tuwalya
to-wahl-yah

soap - sabon
sah-bon

Bathroom
Banyo
bahn-yo

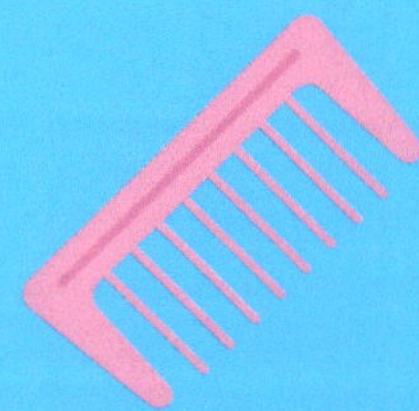

comb - suklay
sook-lie

tub - banyera
ban-yeh-rah

dipper - tabo
tah-boo

tweezer - sipit
see-pit

sleep - tulog
too-log

drink - inom
ee-nom

eat - kain
kah-in

run - takbo
tak-boh

Actions Gawain ga-wah-in

jump - talon
tah-lon

walk - lakad
lah-kad

bath - maligo
mah-lee-goh

study - aral
ah-ral

father - tatay
tah-tie

mother- nanay
nah-nye

grandma - lola
loh-lah

grandpa - lolo
loh-loh

People
Mga Tao
ma-nga tah-o

doctor - doktor
dok-tor

pilot - piloto
pee-loh-toh

engineer - inhinyero
in-hin-yeh-roh

teacher - guro
goo-roh

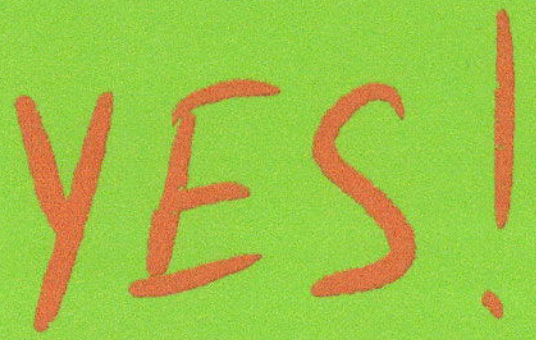

yes - oo
oh-oh

no - hindi
hin-dee

thank you - salamat
sah-lah-mat

welcome - maligayang pagdating
mah-lee-gah-yang pag-dah-ting

Useful Words

Mahalagang Salita

mah-ha-lah-gang sah-lee-tah

good morning - magandang umaga
ma-gahn-dang oo-mah-gah

please - pakiusap
pah-kee-oh-sap

good afternoon - magandang hapon
ma-gahn-dang ha-pohn

good night - magandang gabi
ma-gahn-dang gah-bi

Vehicles
Sasakyan
sah-sak-yan

jeep - dyip
jee-ip

boat - bangka
bang-kah

bus - bus
boos

airplane - eroplano
eh-ro-plah-no

train - tren
tr-eh-n

motorcycle - motorsiklo
mo-tor-seek-lo

ambulance - ambulansya
am-boo-lan-sya

bike - bisikleta
bee-sek-leh-tah

happy - masaya
mah-sah-yah

sad - malungkot
mah-loong-kot

mad - galit
gah-lit

boredom - inip
ee-nip

Feelings
Damdamin
dam-dah-min

tired - pagod
pah-good

scared - takot
tah-kot

excited - sabik
sah-beek

love - mahal
mah-hal

rain - ulan
oo-lahn

wind - hangin
hah-ngin

snow - niyebe
nee-yeh-beh

stormy - bagyo
bag-yoh

Weather
Panahon
pah-na-hon

sunny - maaraw
mah-ah-raw

hot - mainit
mah-ee-nit

cold - malamig
mah-lah-mig

cloudy - maulap
mah-oo-lap

guitar - gitara
gee-tah-rah

trumpet - trompeta
trom-peh-tah

piano - piyano
pee-yah-no

tambourine - pandereta
pahn-deh-reh-tah

Musical Instruments Panugtog pah-nog-tog

drum - tambol
tahm-bol

accordion - akordyon
ah-kor-dyon

xylophone - silopono
see-loh-poh-no

flute - plawta
plaw-tah

school - paaralan
pah-ah-rah-lan

church - simbahan
sim-bah-han

post office - koreo
ko-reh-o

playground - palaruan
pah-lah-roo-ahn

Neighborhood
Purok
poo-rok

store - tindahan
tin-dah-han

hospital - ospital
os-pee-tal

gasoline station - gasolinahan
gah-so-lee-nah-han

police - polisia
po-lee-syah

book - aklat
ahk-lat

calculator -
kalkulador
kal-koo-lah-dor

crayons - krayola
krah-yo-lah

backpack - bag
bag

School
Paaralan
pah-ah-rah-lan

notebook -
kuwaderno
koo-wah-der-noh

pencil - lapis
lah-pis

scissors - gunting
goon-ting

pen - pluma
ploo-mah

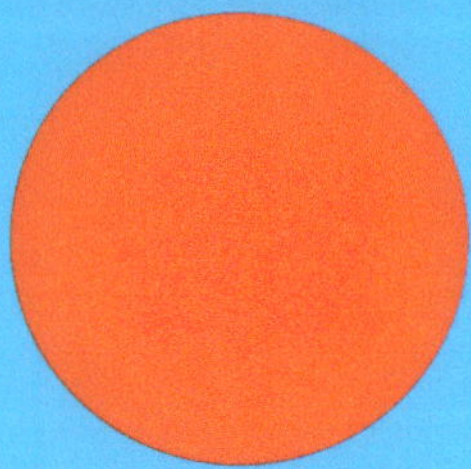

circle - bilog
bee-lohg

triangle - tatsulok
tat-soo-lok

square - parisukat
pah-ree-soo-kat

rectangle - parihaba
pah-ree-hah-bah

Shapes
Hugis
ho-gis

oval - habilog
hah-bee-log

diamond - dyamante
dya-man-teh

pentagon - pentagono
pen-tah-go-noh

heptagon - heptagono
hep-tah-go-noh

You Can Speak Tagalog!

You don’t need perfect grammar.
You don’t need a big vocabulary.
If you can point, smile, and say one word,
you’re already communicating.
Kaya mo ‘yan!
You can do this!

Explore more books by

Jeanette Withington and Edith Withington

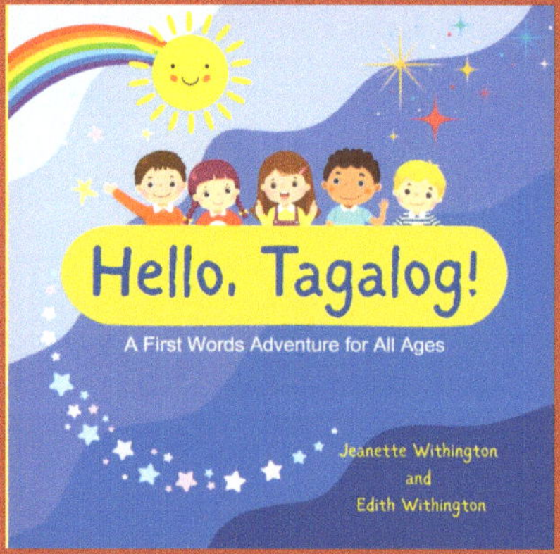

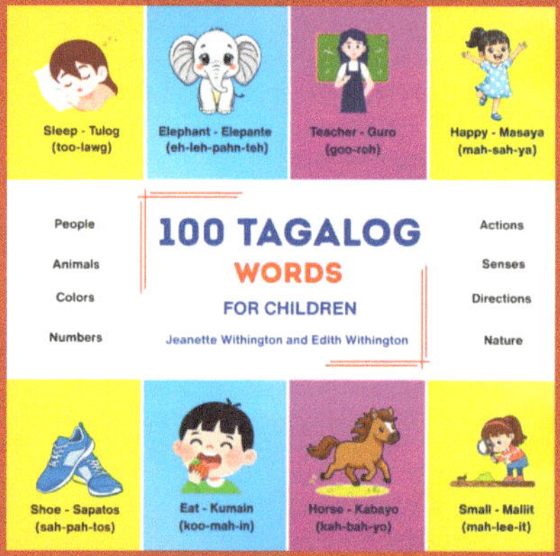

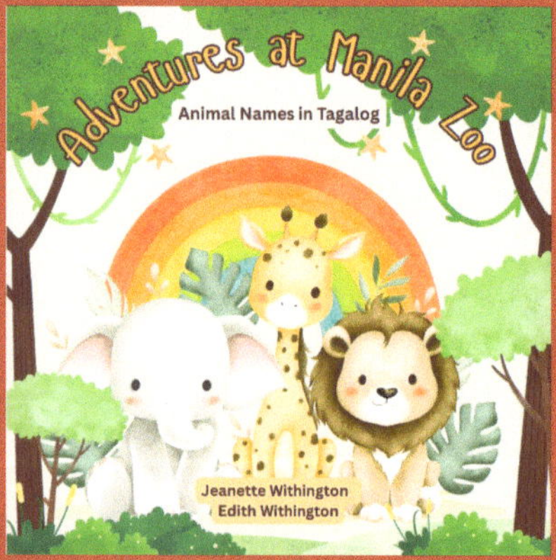

www.ingramcontent.com/pod-product-compliance
Ingram Content Group UK Ltd.
Pitfield, Milton Keynes, MK11 3LW, UK
UKHW061218060826
14089UKWH00046BA/184
* 9 7 9 8 9 9 4 5 3 3 4 5 1 *